KING'S CAPTIVE
The story of Daniel

Belshazzar's feast is brought to a
standstill when strange foreign words,
written by an invisible hand, suddenly
appear on the palace wall. What can they
mean? The wise men and scholars are
baffled. Only Daniel, an exile from
Jerusalem, understands the dreadful
message. Will he dare tell the wicked
king of the doom and destruction that
the writing foretells?

King's Captive

The story of Daniel

Max Bolliger

Translated by Marion Koenig
Illustrated by Edith Schindler

A LION PAPERBACK
Tring • Batavia • Sydney

First edition 1968 Otto Maier Verlag Ravensburg
(published under the title of *Daniel und ein Volk in Gefangenschaft*)
First UK edition 1988

Copyright © 1968 Otto Maier Verlag Ravensburg
Translation copyright © 1970 Dell Publishing Co Inc

This edition published by
Lion Publishing plc
Icknield Way, Tring, Herts, England
ISBN 0 7459 1344 X
Albatross Books Pty Ltd
PO Box 320, Sutherland, NSW 2232, Australia
ISBN 0 86760 949 4

British Library Cataloguing in Publication Data
Bolliger, Max
   King's captive: the story of Daniel.
   1. Daniel — Juvenile literature
   I. Title   II. Schindler, Edith
   III. Daniel und ein Volk in Gefangenschaft.
   English
   224'.509505   BS580.D2
   ISBN 0-7459-1344-X

Printed and bound in Great Britain by
Cox and Wyman, Reading

1

Daniel woke in the middle of the night. He sat up and stared into the darkness.

The narrow windows were barred. He could hear the regular step of a guard outside the door. Beside him, wrapped in blankets, lay his friends. He listened to their breathing. Some stirred, others sighed in their sleep.

Everything that had happened to him in the last few days passed through his mind again: his mother waking him up, his father's worried face, the soldiers marching past his house.

'The enemy are fighting their way into the city. We must flee,' his mother had cried.

They had heard the sound of battle cries, the clash of arms in the streets, and, as he and the rest of the crowd had fought their way out through the city gates, they had suddenly been surrounded by enemy soldiers.

Daniel and his friends were now the prisoners of Nebuchadnezzar, King of Babylon.

Would he ever see his father or brothers and sisters again?

What would become of Jerusalem, his home town?

The prophet Jeremiah had foreseen this disaster and warned the people. Why had the king not taken any notice of his words? He had even laughed at him and locked him up. 'He is a fool,' people had said of the prophet. Only once had Daniel seen Jeremiah, passing in the street. Yet he had never forgotten his face. It had imprinted itself in his mind. Now he could see it before him, and though it was midnight and he felt very much alone, it filled him with comfort and confidence.

Proudly, the victorious king, Nebuchadnezzar, ran his eye over the long line of wagons which were taking the spoils of war — grain, cloth, arms, and horses, but above all, the precious gold and silver treasure from the temple of the alien god — to Babylon.

Ashpenaz, his chief chamberlain, reported to him:

'Many of the enemy were killed during the

battle; King Jehoiakim has been taken prisoner and so have soldiers, workmen, women and children.'

'I need slaves, good workers and strong men,' said Nebuchadnezzar. 'I have vast building plans.'

'And what shall we do with the royal children and those belonging to the chief courtiers?' asked Ashpenaz.

'Jehoiakim is to live at my court as a prisoner. As for the boys — choose the best-looking and most intelligent. Have them taught for three years. Train them to serve me.'

Slowly, Ashpenaz walked past the rows of Judean boys. He asked them to tell him where they were from and tested their knowledge. His eyes rested approvingly on Daniel. He was well built. His eyes were clear and looked intelligent. Thick black hair covered his head like a helmet.

'How old are you?'

'Sixteen, Master.'

'And your name?'

'My name is Daniel. My father was an official at the king's court in Jerusalem.'

Ashpenaz made a sign to the man accompanying him.

'Daniel,' he said, 'I have chosen you to serve at King Nebuchadnezzar's court in Babylon. If you are willing and obedient, no harm shall come to you.'

Daniel was not the only one.

Among the boys that had been chosen, he met Hananiah, Mishael, and Azariah. They had been given new names by Ashpenaz. Hananiah he called Shadrach, Mishael became Meshach, and Azariah, Abednego. Daniel knew all three of them. Their fathers had also worked for the king. They had played and fought together. Now they promised to help each other, to stay loyal to the customs of their people, and not to forget God.

The solemn occasion had made them friends.

It was the duty of Ashpenaz, the chief chamberlain, to see that the foreign boys should lack nothing. They were taught by the best teachers. An overseer took care of their physical welfare. They were given the king's

own wine to drink and his food to eat.

'We are not used to this heavy wine, nor to so much food. Most of it is forbidden to us,' Daniel told his friends. 'I shall ask Ashpenaz to give us only vegetables, fruit and water.'

Ashpenaz listened to Daniel's request. He shook his head. 'Who are you to be dissatisfied?' he asked.

'I know how to value the king's generosity,' Daniel said politely. 'The wine is delicious, but it makes us sleepy. I know the food is carefully chosen, but it makes us lazy.'

Ashpenaz could not be angry with the boy.

But he said: 'Daniel, it was not I who chose your food and drink, but the king. That makes it a command. What would happen if you were to grow less strong than the others? It would cost me my life.'

'How is it that Daniel's eyes, and those of Shadrach, Meshach and Abednego are clearer than those of the other boys?' Ashpenaz asked the overseer, some time later. 'Why are their answers more intelligent and their bodies stronger?'

The overseer blushed. He remained silent. He glanced at Daniel in a questioning way.

Should he tell the chief chamberlain the secret?

He had given in to Daniel's pleading and secretly given the four boys only vegetables, fruit and fresh water for the last ten days.

Ashpenaz noticed his embarrassment.

Suddenly, he laughed.

'I suppose nothing is as good for them as vegetables, fruit and water,' he said. Without asking any further questions, he went away.

Thankfully, Daniel watched him go.

Three years passed. The Jewish boys became young men. The king ordered them to be brought to his throne room. Brightly coloured, finely woven carpets deadened their footsteps. The walls were decorated with alabaster tiles, with drawings and ornaments. The king was depicted in them. He was shown killing elephants and lions with his lance. This strange splendour overawed the prisoners.

Ashpenaz stood behind the king's throne. He signalled to them to come closer.

'These are the Jewish boys,' he said proudly. 'There is not one of them who does not speak our language, not one of them who cannot read or write.'

This was the first time the prisoners had come close to the Babylonian king. His hair fell down to his shoulders. The pointed hat was decorated with precious stones. The square-cut, evenly curled beard reached down over his chest. His hands, covered with rings, rested on the arms of his throne, which was decorated with the heads of bulls and dragons.

Appraisingly, his eyes rested on the young men. Respectfully, they bowed down to kiss his feet.

'Arise.'

Then he turned to Ashpenaz.

'Reading, writing, astronomy, arithmetic and history are not enough,' he said. 'I want to know how wise and intelligent they are. I want to test them.'

What Ashpenaz had said was true. The eyes of Daniel and his friends were clearer than those of the other young men. Their answers were more intelligent, their bodies stronger.

'Daniel, Shadrach, Meshach and Abednego,' said Nebuchadnezzar. 'Your answers to my questions were ten times better than those which the others gave me. You are even wiser than my astrologers and prophets. I want you near me. I shall give you a house next to my palace. You will live there together.'

2

The glimmer of dawn penetrated Nebuchadnezzar's bed chamber. The king got up from his couch and went to the open window. Drops of sweat clung to his forehead. Impatiently he waited for the sun to rise. His lips moved.

'I have been frightened by a dream,' he whispered. 'Am I not one of the mightiest kings in the world? Ships bring me precious goods from distant lands. My treasure chambers are full. Strangers marvel at the produce from my fields. My people love me. And even the lowliest of my slaves need never go to bed hungry. What has made me so afraid?'

Now the first rays of the sun shone over the summit of the hill. On the walls of the main gate of Babylon, dedicated to the goddess Ishtar, there was a gleam like fire. Thousands of coloured glass tiles dazzled the king's eyes.

He sighed.

'If I do not find out what my dream was, I shall have no peace.'

Nebuchadnezzar called together all the wise men and astrologers in his kingdom.

'I have had a dream,' he said. 'I want to know what kind of dream it was.'

'May the king live for ever,' they replied. 'Tell us your dream and we shall tell you its meaning.'

When he heard their words, Nebuchadnezzar's face darkened.

'I have forgotten the dream. You are to tell me what it was. I will reward you handsomely if you do.'

The wise men were afraid. Had they understood the king rightly?

The oldest among them spoke:

'No king, however mighty he may be, can demand from his servants what only the gods know. But tell us your dream and we will tell you its meaning.'

The king flared out at them.

'How dare you talk to me like that! Tell me my dream or I will pull down your houses and have you cut to pieces.'

'Does the king realize he is demanding the impossible from his wise men?'

'Wise men! Liars and boasters, that's all you are! Get out of my sight! I never want to see you again.'

Frightened and outraged, the astrologers and wise men fled from the palace.

The king brooded silently.

'Of what use are might and wealth to me?' he thought.

However hard he tried, he could not remember his dream. Fear gnawed at him like a cruel beast.

In his desperation, he called Arioch, the captain of the guard, into his presence.

'Take 100 soldiers,' he ordered, 'and fetch all the astrologers and wise men to my palace. I have had enough of their fine words. I shall have them all put to death.'

'And what about the four young men from Judah?' asked Arioch. 'Has the King not found them wiser than all his learned men?'

'I am sure they will not be able to tell me my dream either.'

'But they are innocent,' Arioch reminded the king.

Nebuchadnezzar was adamant.

'They shall be put to death. Arrest them and bring them here.'

Daniel and his friends were at work calculating the course of the stars and deciphering ancient scripts.

Arioch knocked on their door.

'What brings you to us? Is it an order from the king?' asked Daniel. He was startled to see the armed soldiers behind their captain.

'Yes, an order from the king,' said Arioch quietly. 'I must take you to prison. You have been condemned to death.'

He explained what had happened at the palace.

'No one can change this ill fortune,' he said.

Daniel listened attentively.

What was going on in his mind? His eyes were looking far away. As on the first night he had spent in prison, he could see Jeremiah's face in his mind's eye.

'Daniel, what is the matter with you? Speak!'

'Arioch, lead me to the king. I will try to help him,' he said in a determined voice.

Sleepless nights had made Nebuchad-nezzar's face pale and drawn. Daniel could hardly recognize him.

'What do you want?' asked the king.

'Arioch has told me what is troubling you. I will ask God to help me find your dream.'

The king laughed mockingly. 'What kind of god is that?'

Daniel was not to be diverted from his purpose.

'The God of Judah, the invisible God of my people,' he said.

Something in Daniel's voice made the king pay closer attention. He looked into Daniel's eyes. He was reminded of the day when the boys from Judah had first been led before him, when he had found this one wiser and more handsome than all the others. He smiled.

'Daniel, you awaken new hope,' he said.

'I will wait three days for your answer. Woe betide you, however, if this respite should prove to have been in vain.'

After his talk with the king, Daniel returned to his friends.

He asked them to leave him alone. 'Pray,'

he said. 'Our lives are in God's hand.'

In solitude, he listened to the silence. It helped to prepare him for God's voice.

'Daniel! Daniel! Daniel!'

He trembled.

'Daniel, I will give you the power to understand deep and secret things. I shall give you the gift of interpreting dreams. Go to Nebuchadnezzar. I will put the right words in your mouth.'

Daniel had fallen on to his knees.

'Lord, thy will be done,' he whispered.

God's voice filled his whole being like a strong current.

With shining eyes he returned to his friends three days later.

'God is great,' he said quietly.

'God has revealed to me what we have prayed for. He knows all that is deep and hidden. He knows what lies in the darkness.'

It was not only the king, but also Arioch and the imprisoned wise men and astrologers who waited anxiously for Daniel's reply.

Would this reply save them?

At the appointed time, Daniel appeared

before the king.

Nebuchadnezzar had sent the guards, ministers, and even his chief chamberlain away. He was alone with Daniel.

'Speak,' he ordered him.

'My King, there is a God in heaven who knows all that is hidden. He is the invisible God of my fathers. It is he who speaks to you in my words. And this was your dream: You saw a great image standing before you. Its head was of fine gold, its breast and arms were of silver, its belly was of brass. Its legs were made of iron and its feet were half iron and half clay. Suddenly a stone fell from where you did not know. It broke the feet of iron and clay. The gigantic image crashed to the ground and dissolved like chaff before the wind. The stone, however, grew into a mountain which filled the world.'

The king had followed his words with breathless interest.

'Yes, that was my dream. Go on.'

'Now I will tell you its meaning,' Daniel went on. 'The dream showed you the future. You, Nebuchadnezzar, are the head made of gold. God has given you might and strength. After your death no kingdom will surpass yours for splendour. One kingdom will be like silver, another like brass, another only iron. The last one, however, will be a divided kingdom.'

'And what does the stone represent?'

'The stone which fell from heaven represents God's strength. He will raise a kingdom that will be eternal and will fill the whole world.'

While Daniel had been speaking, the king had risen from his throne. Slowly, he had descended step by step.

'Daniel,' he said. 'Through you, I have found out the thoughts in my heart.'

In his robes of state, with his crown and sceptre, Nebuchadnezzar appeared before his assembled ministers, wise men, astrologers and courtiers the next day.

Beside him stood Daniel.

'Daniel has revealed my dream to me and interpreted it,' announced the king. 'I have found peace through him. There is no doubt: his God is a God of gods and a King of kings. Take note: I have raised Daniel above all my wise men and astrologers. I wished to make him ruler over the whole province of Babylon

but he declined this office. Instead, I have appointed Shadrach, Meshach and Abednego to rule over the province, for I have found them wise and just. Daniel, however, will stay here at court by my side.'

A sigh of relief ran through the hall.

'May the King live for ever!'

'Long live Daniel!'

Only the wise men and astrologers, who had been set free from their imprisonment, remained silent.

'The king has set a young man over us. Three prisoners from Judah are to rule over Babylon,' they muttered.

They had already forgotten that Daniel had saved their lives.

3

An image three score cubits high and six score cubits wide was to make known to the world the fame of Nebuchadnezzar, the King of Babylon.

It had been set up in the plain of Dura, near the capital of Babylon.

In the streets and market-places people could talk of nothing else.

One man said to another, 'It is made of solid gold.'

All the most important men in Babylon had been invited to the dedication of the image: princes, governors, captains, judges and treasurers.

'They must all worship my splendour,' said the king.

A cloudless blue sky stretched overhead.

In bright, festive robes, the guests crowded round the shrouded image.

'Silence! The royal heralds are announcing a decree from the king.'

'Hear, O people! When the sound of the trumpet, flute, harp and psaltery rings out, you will fall down and worship the golden image. Whoever disobeys the king's decree shall be cast into the midst of a burning, fiery furnace.'

Suddenly a movement rang through the crowd. Universal rejoicing filled the air.

Trumpets announced the king's arrival.

'May the King live for ever!'

'Long live the King! His fame is known throughout the world. His might is great.'

Contentedly, Nebuchadnezzar leaned back in his upholstered seat. Full of awe, the people in the crowd drew back from his state carriage, drawn by eight horses. The king smiled and waved to the crowd. He wore splendid clothes: a long purple tunic made of silk. His wrists were hung with golden bracelets. The handle of his dagger was encrusted with precious stones. A costly earring glittered in the sunlight.

Nebuchadnezzar stopped in front of the

image. Solemnly he stepped up on to the platform which had been erected for him. A servant followed him carrying the great sunshade.

For the last time a herald announced the king's decree:

'When the sound of the trumpet, flute, harp, and psaltery rings out, you shall fall down and worship the image.'

It had grown still. The wind could be heard rustling the trees, and in the distance rose the startled cry of a bird.

Thousands of eyes were fixed on the king. The musicians and dancers stood ready.

At a sign from the king, the veil fell.

Silent, glittering in the sunshine, the image reared up over the kneeling crowds. The face of the image bore the king's proud features.

But what was the matter with the wise men and astrologers? They were exchanging glances and whispering to each other: 'Look at the young men from Judah!'

'There they are, standing up in the midst of kneeling people.'

'Shadrach, Meshach and Abednego have

dared to ignore the king's command.'

'We shall denounce them to the king.'

'He will not spare them.'

'Now their power is over.'

'Not even Daniel can save them from the burning fiery furnace.'

'Has someone dared to ignore my command? Who is it?' Nebuchadnezzar demanded angrily.

'O King! If we could only give you better news. They are the three Judeans whom you have made rulers over Babylon: Daniel's friends. They do not worship your gods and refuse to bow down to the golden image.'

The blood rose into the king's face.

'Bring them before me,' he ordered.

Modestly, but fearlessly, Shadrach, Meshach and Abednego stood before the king.

'Why did you ignore my command?' he asked them.

'Lord King, you are great and mighty. You have entrusted us, your prisoners from Judah, with high office. We are grateful to you. But we can never bow down before a golden image.'

This fearless reply made the king thoughtful.

Perhaps he remembered the words Daniel spoke when he was interpreting the dream.

Perhaps he wanted to spare them the terrible punishment for Daniel's sake.

Paying no attention to the outraged glances of the wise men and astrologers, he said, 'I will grant you your lives, if you will now go and kneel to the image.'

'Lord King, you have heard our answer. We cannot change our minds. If God wills, he can even save us from the burning, fiery furnace.'

The king was speechless.

Triumphant, his wise men and astrologers watched him.

The king raged.

His face changed. He looked terrible in his fury.

'Bind them at once! Arioch, heat the furnace seven times hotter than it has ever been. They shall rue their obstinacy and die miserably this very day.'

The king stopped the festivities.

Full of vengeful thoughts, he returned to Babylon. His warriors followed, bringing with them the three bound men.

'The Judean prisoners shall see what happens to those who ignore my commands!'

On his arrival at the citadel he called Daniel into his presence.

'Your friends have ignored my commands. They have repaid my kindness with obstinacy and arrogance. Now I shall see them burn with my own eyes. You, Daniel, shall witness it,' he said.

Daniel was aghast. He knew there was no point in reasoning with the king.

He had been blinded by anger.

The three prisoners from Judah were to be publicly burned.

The big square in front of the king's palace could scarcely hold the crowds of people. The wise men and astrologers who had borne witness against Shadrach, Meshach and Abednego could not conceal their joy.

'Now we have won back the king's favour,' they said.

Above the furnace, which was used for tiles, the air shimmered. The heat scorched the hair and skin of the servants tending the fire.

Daniel stood beside the angry king.

He wished he could have said a word to his friends.

But the king had forbidden him to speak to them.

Shadrach, Meshach and Abednego lay on the ground guarded by soldiers. They did not utter one word of complaint.

'The furnace is ready,' Arioch announced to the king.

Flames as high as a house shot up to the sky.

'Throw them in, bound and dressed, just as they are . . .' ordered Nebuchadnezzar.

'Leave the door open. I want to see their god coming to rescue them,' he mocked.

Shadrach, Meshach and Abednego were dragged up to the furnace, seized by their hands and feet, and thrown into the fire. The heat was so great that it prevented the guards from breathing and stopped them from moving back in time. Not one of them was able to save himself. They fell to the ground, dead.

'Daniel, do you really believe your god can save a man from that heat?' whispered the king hoarsely.

Daniel did not answer.

He was praying.

The crowd had fallen silent.

There was a sound of crackling and roaring.

'If the guards fell dead so quickly, Shadrach, Meshach and Abednego must have died long ago,' said the people. 'We might as well go home.' But what was that?

Out of the fire a voice called: 'I praise you, O Lord God of our fathers. Glorious is your name! We shall follow you with all our hearts. You have saved us with your might. May your enemies see that there is none more powerful than you.'

Nebuchadnezzar flinched. The voice filled him with fear and amazement. He clutched the arms of his chair and leaned forward, staring into the fire. Suddenly, he seized Daniel's arm.

'Am I dreaming, or has the heat turned my brain? I don't just see three figures, I see four of them. They are walking about in the flames as if a fresh breeze were cooling them.'

The king looked round for his guards. But in their faces he read the same horror that he also felt.

Daniel recognized Shadrach's voice.

He sensed that the fourth figure was that of an angel.

And, as if in answer to the people's disbelieving amazement, the voices of Shadrach, Meshach and Abednego now rang out; a song rose up to heaven:

> 'O you sun, moon, and stars,
> And all you winds;
> You grasses and dew,
> Flowers of the earth,
> Mountains and hills;
> All you beasts
> And fishes that move in the water,
> You fowl of the air,
> Bless the Lord.
> O you seas and rivers,
> Light and darkness,
> Thunder, lightning,
> Ice and cold,
> Frost and snow,
> Fire and heat;
> You fountains, too,

Bless the Lord.
O you sons of men,
Bless the Lord.
Give thanks to the God of gods,
For his mercy endureth for ever.'

The king listened, deeply impressed.

He stood up before the marvelling throng.

'Shadrach, Meshach and Abednego,' he called. 'You servants of the highest God, come here to me. Praise be to your God. I know of no other god who could accomplish such a thing. You trusted in him and he has saved you. I, too, shall bless and praise him.'

Unharmed, Shadrach, Meshach and Abednego stepped before the king.

The people crowded round. They touched the young men and felt their clothes.

It was a miracle. It could not be explained rationally.

'Leave them alone,' said Nebuchadnezzar.

He embraced the three men.

After what had happened there was no need for words.

The heralds who had proclaimed the king's command at the start of the festivities were sent out once more.

'This news shall be made known throughout my kingdom,' said Nebuchadnezzar.

'Shadrach, Meshach and Abednego, you shall return to your post as rulers of Babylon. Anyone who blasphemes or mocks the God of the Judean prisoners shall be severely punished.'

Humiliated and angry, the wise men and astrologers hurried away.

4

Nine years had passed since Nebuchadnezzar had conquered Judah. For nine years Daniel had been living in Babylon.

He had not forgotten those of his people who had stayed behind in Judah. Nebuchadnezzar had set governors and overseers over them. He had even given them a king. He was called Zedekiah.

Now although Zedekiah had had to swear loyalty and obedience to the Babylonian king, he had secretly allied himself to the king of Egypt. With Egypt's help, he hoped to conquer Babylon and kill Nebuchadnezzar. He, too, did not heed the warnings given by the prophet Jeremiah.

But his plan failed.

Before the two kings could raise up an army, Nebuchadnezzar had heard of the plan.

His anger was unbounded.

'I have treated my subjects kindly so far, but now I shall show no mercy,' he stormed.

For the second time, he set off against Judah at the head of a vast army. His soldiers had been ordered not to spare anything or anyone.

In towns and villages they acted with the utmost cruelty. Thousands of people were killed and thousands taken prisoner. Zedekiah tried to defend Jerusalem and Nebuchadnezzar's army besieged the city. After a year, hunger forced the Jewish soldiers to surrender.

Nebuchadnezzar made good his threat.

His warriors went through the city plundering, burning, and murdering. The temple built of cedar wood, the king's palace, and those of his nobles, went up in flames. Zedekiah had to watch his children put to death. He himself was brought to Babylon and thrown into prison. There his eyes were put out. He would repent his rebellion against the might of Babylon to the end of his days.

When the Babylonian soldiers left, Jerusalem was just a heap of rubble. All day long,

black clouds of smoke rose up into the sky.

Through the empty alleys, between the piles of stones and heaps of masonry of the wrecked town, walked a man. He leaned on a stick. His face was blackened by smoke, his strength exhausted. Yet he never stopped comforting the dying and searching for the wounded.

He was the prophet Jeremiah.

'No harm shall come to him,' Nebuchadnezzar had ordered his soldiers. 'Look after him.'

At the sight of the city, Jeremiah's heart filled with grief. His prophecies about Jerusalem's fall had come true. Mournfully he cried:

'O Jerusalem,
With whom shall I compare you?
The streets lie desolate
No one moves abroad.
Your destruction is as great as the sea.
Who can heal you?
Judah has been carried into captivity
And weary servitude.
That is why I weep.
The old men no longer sit in the gateway,

And the young men no longer play the lute.
The joy of our hearts has ceased.
Our dance is turned into mourning.'

Once again a great many of the survivors were carried away into Babylon. There were nearly 10,000 of them — once-rich citizens, artisans, and labourers.

Daniel met them everywhere: in the fields, in the workshops, and on the building sites. Most of them did the lowly work of slaves.

The sight of them made Daniel sad.

Many of his countrymen distrusted him.

'He is the king's friend,' they muttered. 'He is treated well.'

Daniel understood their bitterness.

Whenever he could, he tried to ease their hardship.

He found them under the willows by the river when the day's work was done, longing for their homeland.

Babylonian people joined them there. 'Sing us some of your songs,' they begged. 'They sound strange and beautiful to us.'

But the prisoners shook their heads.

'How can we be cheerful and sing?' they replied. 'Our harps hang on the willows with

broken strings.'

'When shall we return home? How long must we be slaves?' they kept asking Daniel over and over again.

'Yes. How long?'

'Only God knows,' he replied, but his heart was full of doubts and questions.

Since his friends had been ruling over the province of Babylon, Daniel had lived alone in the house which the king had given them.

'Master, there is a man outside,' his servant announced to him one day. 'He seems to have come a long way and he will talk only to you.'

'Bring him in,' said Daniel.

The stranger was exhausted. His clothes were covered with dust.

He held out a scroll to Daniel.

'Where do you come from?' asked Daniel.

'From the ruined city, Jerusalem. Jeremiah sent me.'

'Jeremiah!'

Hurriedly, Daniel rolled open the scroll.

His hands shook.

'God has spoken to me,' wrote Jeremiah. 'The captivity will last another fifty years. It is a long time, but God will not forsake you. Do not try to avoid your destiny. Build houses and plant gardens. Work hard and you will not fare badly, even in an alien land.'

Daniel knew what these words meant. They were also intended for him.

He determined to care for the prisoners more than ever, to be a comfort and help to them. The people must not grow tired of telling their children about Judah. God must stay alive in their hearts.

The messenger was still standing in front of Daniel.

He did not dare to disturb Daniel's thoughts. At last Daniel rolled up the scroll.

'Go and rest,' he said to the man. 'My servant will look after you.'

Daniel went to his room. He opened the chest containing his few treasures: a boy's torn clothing — he had worn it on his flight from Jerusalem; a leather belt with a silver clasp — it was a present from his father; a small harp which someone had brought to him from his homeland; a round, smoothly worn stone from the valley where the shepherd boy who became King David once had fought against the giant Goliath. Daniel smiled at his simple treasures. They were all he owned. Now he laid the precious letter among them.

'Lord,' he prayed, 'give me strength. From now on, my whole life belongs to you.'

Nebuchadnezzar's wrath against the rebellious Jews had died down after his great victory.

There was peace in the land.

The many slaves from Judah were most useful to the king.

'I want to make Babylon the biggest, most beautiful city in the world,' he said.

For this he needed workmen.

New palaces and temples grew up. Beside his citadel, he had gardens laid out in overhanging terraces. They seemed to be floating in the air. People called them 'hanging gardens'.

Strangers walked, marvelling, under the gigantic triumphal arch and down the broad, straight streets. In no other city in the world was so much business done, in no other city were so many festivals celebrated.

A double wall, equipped with strong turrets, surrounded the city.

'Nothing can harm me,' Nebuchadnezzar announced triumphantly, standing on the highest pinnacle of his palace. 'My might is as great as that of the gods.'

'My might is as great as that of the gods.' Had Nebuchadnezzar forgotten the miracle in the burning, fiery furnace?

'Silence,' he commanded, when Daniel reminded him. 'Pray to your invisible god, but leave me in peace. Never fear, I shall not forget what you have done for me.'

But one day, when Daniel met him, the king was deep in thought.

'My King, what is troubling you?'

'A dream,' said Nebuchadnezzar. 'Daniel, I have made you the chief of all my wise men and astrologers. I will tell you my dream. You shall interpret it. I saw a mighty tree, which had a human heart. It reached up to the sky and its branches spread out over the whole world. They were fine branches and bore fruit. All the animals in the world found shade under the tree and the birds lived among its leaves. Then, suddenly, an angel flew down from heaven and gave orders that the tree should be cut down and its branches

stripped away. The animals ran away and the birds fled. "Leave the stump," said the angel. "Bind it with iron chains, take away its human heart, and for seven months give it that of an animal instead." '

'O my King,' said Daniel sadly. 'If only this dream had been dreamed by one of your enemies and not you.'

The king grew afraid.

'Speak,' he said. 'Interpret the dream. I am not afraid of the truth.'

'You, my King, are this tree,' said Daniel. 'You are great and mighty, and your power stretches to the ends of the world. But God wants you to recognize that his might is even greater than yours. He will test you. You are about to suffer a serious illness.'

Daniel's words came true.

Nebuchadnezzar's reason became clouded. From his mouth came only insane gibberish. His eyes shone with a mad light.

'An evil spirit has entered him,' said the doctors and healers. 'We cannot help him.'

One morning, the king vanished from the palace. People saw him drifting through the woods and fields like a ghost. He ate grass

and roots like an animal. He slept in caves and under trees.

His once magnificent robes hung from him in rags. His hair resembled eagles' feathers, and his nails, the claws of birds. At the sight of him the people were filled with terror and fled.

Belshazzar, his son, now ruled in the palace.

If he could, he would already have had himself proclaimed king.

'It is bad for a country to be without a king,' the ministers said, too.

Daniel warned them against taking this step.

'The king is not dead, the king is ill.'

'How dare you, a prisoner from Judah, talk to us like that,' said Belshazzar.

He looked at Daniel with hatred in his eyes.

But Daniel would not give way. He had not forgotten the king's dream.

'Leave the stump rooted in the ground; bind it with iron chains, take away its human heart, and for seven months give it that of an animal.'

Daniel knew that the king would return.

The king did return. With few words, he took up his old duties and work again. His eyes were clear in the pale, sunken face. Full of shame, Belshazzar and the ministers lowered their eyes.

The king was well again.

'Long live the King! Long live Nebuchadnezzar!'

Over and over again this cry rose up outside the walls of the palace.

The people wanted to see their king. The square in front of the palace was crowded.

Nebuchadnezzar walked over to the windows.

He waved at the crowds. He smiled.

A sigh of relief rippled through the square.

Daniel stood beside him.

'Daniel,' said the king quietly. 'Now I know that there is only one God and no other gods besides him. I was proud and have become humble. I have found peace. From now on I will serve him.'

5

After he had recovered from his illness, Nebuchadnezzar reigned for an additional ten years. They were happy years, not just for the Babylonians, but also for the prisoners from Judah. The king ordered houses to be built for them and gardens laid out. The conscientious workers and good business-men were valued by the Babylonians.

What Jeremiah had written came to pass.

Then Nebuchadnezzar's death hit the people like a thunderbolt.

They could not grasp it. Nebuchadnezzar, the great king, was dead!

Sorrowfully, uneasily, they gathered in the streets.

Wailing, the soldiers marched past the stone coffin containing the body of the king.

Daniel also mourned his death.

'God's power was first revealed to me through you. Daniel, I have loved you like my own son.'

Those were the last words Daniel ever heard Nebuchadnezzar say.

Daniel was no longer young. He had been living at the court of Babylon for thirty-five years. Many of those who had loved him were dead, including Ashpenaz, the chamberlain, and Arioch, the captain of the king's guard.

Daniel thought of Jeremiah's letter and his prophecies.

From Egypt had come news of his death.

Nebuchadnezzar's dream of the image with the golden head and the feet of iron and clay came true. Every year Babylon's might became weaker.

Belshazzar, Nebuchadnezzar's eldest son, cared neither for the welfare of his people nor for the defence of his land. Instead, news quickly spread abroad of his wild celebrations and feasting. The gods of gold, silver, stone, and wood were worshipped once again. Their ruined temples were rebuilt.

The Jewish prisoners soon felt the force of

Belshazzar's severity. 'They led Nebuchadnezzar astray with this invisible god of theirs. They were treated much too leniently,' he said.

Shadrach, Meshach and Abednego barely escaped his persecution.

They sought refuge with Daniel.

'Flee! Hide yourself away in the country before Belshazzar is reminded of your existence,' they advised him.

Daniel calmed them down.

'Has God ever forsaken us while we believed in him? I shall not run away. We must stick it out. The bad times will soon be over. You must help me. The prisoners will need us more than ever now. Go to them. They must not forget that God loves us, although he is punishing us with this long captivity. Give them courage.'

Strengthened by Daniel's words, the three set out. Belshazzar had dismissed them from their positions as rulers of the Babylonian province. But God had now chosen them for a greater service.

In the king's palace a great feast was taking place. Belshazzar had invited 1,000 of his

friends — governors, courtiers, chiefs, warriors and priests.

In the light of the torches and candles, the coloured robes gleamed, the precious stones glittered and sparkled.

Musicians played their instruments. Dancers entertained the guests.

Servants carried in great platters of roast meat, fish, poultry, and vegetables. Others filled the great pitchers with rare wines. Mountains of fresh fruit and bowls of sweet pastries lined the tables.

Belshazzar could hardly remain upright in his chair. He stared at his full goblet with glassy eyes.

'The Judeans shall get to know me better. I will write with their blood,' he mumbled.

'Hail to Belshazzar! Hail! Hail!' shouted the guests. Their shouts urged the king to worse blasphemies.

'Tell me, who is this invisible God? Come here, you God of Judah. Let me see you. Are you made of air? Come here and show me your strength.'

'Hail to Belshazzar! Hail! Hail! Our gods are the true gods,' replied the guests.

The king laughed loudly.

'Are not our treasure chambers full of the treasure from Jerusalem's temple? Ho, Treasurer, bring them here, the golden candlesticks, the goblets and bowls. We want to drink out of them.'

The old keeper of the treasure chamber paled.

Were they not holy vessels? Had not Nebuchadnezzar taught them to honour this god?

'What are you waiting for?' Belshazzar yelled at him. 'Bring the treasure here at once.'

Two servants carried the tray on which the beautifully wrought vessels lay.

'Put them here on the table,' ordered Belshazzar.

With his own hands, he filled the goblets and bowls with wine.

What did it matter that half of it was spilled?

He was the first to raise a golden goblet.

'Hail to the invisible god of our slaves,' he shouted mockingly. 'Come, we will all . . .'

He stopped in mid-sentence.

His face became distorted. His eyes stared at the wall.

Full of horror, his guests followed the direction of his eyes.

An invisible hand was slowly writing large letters on the wall.

Out of the letters grew words.

Who could read them?

They were in a foreign language.

The king shrank down into his chair.

He trembled.

'What is that?' he whispered in the uncanny silence.

Was he crazed with drink?

Was it only a ghostly apparition, an optical illusion?

No. Vivid and clear, the words stood written on the wall:

MENE MENE TEKEL PARSIN

'Fetch the wise men and scholars,' ordered the king. 'They shall decipher this script and tell me its meaning.' His voice failed him.

'Wake them up! Hurry!' he whispered weakly.

The wise men and scholars stared at the writing on the wall, baffled.

'Whoever can read this writing and tell me what it means shall be dressed in scarlet. I will give him a golden chain and he shall be the third ruler in the kingdom,' promised the king. But not one of the wise men could solve the riddle.

In their eyes the king read the reflection of his own fear.

He sent them away.

He looked round desperately.

The candles flickered. Gigantic shadows moved on the wall. The food had grown cold on the plates and dishes. No one refilled the half-empty goblets.

Terrified, full of horror, most of the guests had slipped away.

'Daniel!'

It was the queen mother who had suddenly remembered his existence.

'My King,' she said. 'Do not be so afraid. I know of a man in your kingdom who can help you. He used to interpret your father's dreams and reveal the meaning of hidden words. Nebuchadnezzar raised him above all the wise men and astrologers and scholars. Daniel. You must send for him!'

For a long time the king remained silent.

'Daniel.'

He had not seen him since the death of King Nebuchadnezzar.

'Very well,' he said. 'Bring him here to me.'

It was long past midnight.

Calmly Daniel walked across to the palace beside the king's messenger.

He was not afraid.

'My God,' he prayed. 'Grant that I may say the right words to your enemy.'

The king greeted him in silence.

Only a few faithful servants had remained with him.

A light, which seemed to shine from Daniel's face, confused the king.

'Daniel, you whom my father brought here from Judah, read and interpret the writing on the wall for me. If you do, I will dress you in scarlet. I will give you a golden chain and you shall be the third ruler in the kingdom.'

Daniel saw the writing. He saw the remains of the king's feast, and, on the table, the treasure from God's temple.

The sight of them filled him with sorrow.

'Belshazzar,' he said. 'Keep your gifts or give them to someone else. I want neither

riches nor might. Your father was a proud and powerful king and he became humble before God. But you, Belshazzar, who knew all this, prayed to the golden, silver, stone, and wooden gods; you have drunk out of the holy goblets and mocked and blasphemed the living God who gives life to all things. I will now read the writing and interpret it to you. God has written it on the wall.

MENE MENE TEKEL PARSIN

That means, "measured, measured, weighed, divided." The days of your kingdom are numbered. God has weighed you and found you too light. Your kingdom will be conquered and divided by the Medes and Persians.'

Daniel had hardly finished speaking when the wall became as white as it had been before.

Did the king, in his drunken stupor, take in the terrible prophecy? Should he not, now, fall down and beg God for forgiveness?

'I will keep my promise,' he said. 'Bring me a scarlet robe and a golden chain. And tomorrow I will make you the third ruler of my kingdom.'

Before the servant could return with the robe and chain, Daniel had disappeared.

Silently, he returned to his home.

Already the sky was growing pink towards the east. Soon the sun would rise, and with it a new day. What would it bring?

The people of Babylon awoke.

The guards opened the city gates to the farmers and dealers. Their two-wheeled carts were laden with flowers, fruit, and vegetables. Fresh eggs lay packed in baskets. Lambs bleated in narrow cages.

The weavers, potters, smiths, and carpenters opened the doors of their workshops.

On the towers and pinnacles of the king's citadel shone the first rays of the rising sun. The soldiers guarding the entrance rubbed their eyes sleepily. They could rest in peace. The captain would not be coming for a long time. He had been invited to the king's feast.

But all of a sudden the door was thrust open from inside.

A rider shot out. It was the captain.

He was followed by heavily armed soldiers.

The guards stared at them, flabbergasted.

What had happened?

'Belshazzar is dead! He has been found murdered in his bedchamber!'

Like wildfire, the news spread through the town.

Who was the murderer? Was it one of the Jewish prisoners? Or one of his own servants?

Or a spy from the Medes and Persians, the enemies living on their borders? Hadn't they long been waiting for just such a moment? Perhaps their armies were already marching towards the city.

The people barred themselves into their houses.

The market stayed empty. The flowers withered.

6

A battle was fought on the frontier. The Babylonian army tried to beat back the Medes and Persians. But King Belshazzar's murder seemed to weaken the soldiers. What were they fighting for? Their resistance was poor.

Towns and villages surrendered willingly.

After five days the enemy conquerors moved into the capital city and took possession of the royal citadel.

Their red flags flew from the turrets.

Belshazzar's body was buried in the garden without ceremony. No one mourned for him.

'I have been received in Babylon not as an enemy but as a friend and saviour,' said Cyrus, the king of the Persians, writing home to his own country. 'I have freed the inhabitants of Babylon from a yoke. I, Cyrus, the greatest king in the four quarters of the world.' The king of the Medes was called Darius. Cyrus was greater in power and standing than he. But they were allies.

Darius was sixty-two years old.

He had taken over the government of the conquered kingdom.

'Find me 120 wise and honest men. I will set them to govern the provinces,' he told his ministers.

Darius had also heard of Daniel, of his wisdom and the power he had to interpret dreams and the hidden meanings of words. Nobody had forgotten the writing on the wall. It had made Daniel famous. People talked of him with awe and respect.

'God speaks to us through him,' said the prisoners from Judah. 'He is a prophet.'

Darius sent for him.

He wanted to meet the man about whom so many wonderful things were said.

Daniel did not seek outward fame. Modestly he stood before the new ruler.

Darius sensed Daniel's strength.

'Will you take on a heavy task?' he asked Daniel.

'Yes,' replied Daniel. 'If God has willed it

so. What is it?'

'I wish to set you above the 120 governors and princes of Babylon. You shall be my viceroy.'

Daniel was shocked.

Since Nebuchadnezzar's death, he had lived only for God and his people. Was he now to take on an appointment which would make him the equal of a king?

Because of Jeremiah's letter, Daniel knew that the Judeans' captivity was nearing its end. Now the prisoners would need someone who could intercede for them with the king.

He accepted the task which Darius offered him. But he soon discovered how hard it was.

'Are we to be commanded by Daniel?' cried several of the Babylonian princes and governors.

Envy gnawed at their hearts. Each one of them would have liked to be in Daniel's position.

'Can't we find something bad about him to tell Darius?' they asked.

Daniel did not realize that everything he did was watched by them.

Every morning he came to meetings of the

king and ministers. In the afternoon he visited his countrymen, Jewish priests and friends. And three times a day he could be heard uttering his prayers at the open windows of his balcony. They could find nothing wrong in his behaviour.

'We must set a trap for him and the king,' they said. They plotted together to put Daniel into a situation which would cost him his life.

One day they appeared before Darius.

'All people know how mighty you are, O King, and that your justice is equal to that of the gods,' they said, in a tone of flattery.

'What do you want?' asked Darius.

'We beg you to issue a decree that for thirty days no one may pray to anyone but you. This will test the people's faith.'

One of the princes held out a written tablet to him. 'We have already written down the decree,' he said.

'For thirty days no one may pray to any god or man, except the king. Whoever fails to obey this decree shall be thrown into a den of lions.' All Darius had to add was his name.

'So be it. I will sign your decree,' he said, reaching for his stylus.

Their flattering words had deceived him.

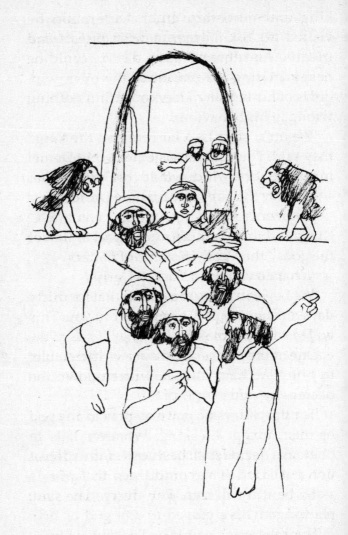

The princes and governors were jubilant.

The king had fallen into the trap. A decree, bearing his signature, could not, according to the law, be countermanded.

The decree was made known throughout the kingdom.

'What a strange decree it is,' thought Daniel. But he had no suspicions. He did not have the faintest idea that this decree was intended only for him, that the princes and governors were seeking his life.

When Daniel said his prayers, with his face towards Jerusalem, his voice could be heard in the street.

Daniel knew that he was disobeying the decree by saying his prayers.

'Do you hear that?' said the servants of the conspirators whom their masters had sent to spy on him. 'Can you hear him begging God to stand by the people of Judah? If he denies it in front of the king, we shall bear witness against him.'

'Daniel,' said Darius, 'several of the princes and governors have complained that you do not obey my decree. For thirty days you should not have prayed to any god or man except me.'

'My King,' replied Daniel, 'when you appointed me your viceroy, I prayed to God to stand by me. How could I do my work without his help?'

'How much you must love your god if not even a savage punishment will stop you from praying to him. It can cost you your life.'

'I respect you, my King, but God has taken from me all awe of mankind. I am not afraid.'

Thoughtfully, without ill will, the king looked at him.

'I will try to save you,' he said quietly.

Now the king knew that the princes and governors had set a trap for him.

They insisted that the punishment be carried out.

'How much longer will you wait? He has not obeyed your decree. He must be thrown to the lions.'

If the king did not carry out his signed command, his princes threatened to revolt.

At the entrance to the lions' den, he laid his hand on Daniel's shoulder.

'Your enemies have outwitted me. I cannot save you.'

'I am not afraid,' said Daniel.

He heard the roar of the hungry animals.

He saw the immense block of stone which the princes and governors had brought to close the entrance. They were afraid that otherwise someone might rescue him. They had not forgotten the angel in the burning, fiery furnace.

'May the God whom you have served all your life help you,' said the king.

Daniel made no resistance when the guards seized him.

Silently Darius returned to the citadel. He knew that Daniel was innocent.

'Did I try everything I could to save him from his enemies?' he kept asking himself.

He touched neither food nor drink.

He could not sleep.

The guards could hear him groaning.

When day began to dawn, he got up and left the palace.

The soldiers at the entrance started to their feet.

He took no notice of their astonished glances.

He was drawn to the lions' den.

The square in front of it was empty. The interior of the den still lay in darkness.

Darius leaned over the balustrade. His voice trembled.

'Daniel! Daniel! Are you still alive?' he called down into the eerie silence.

'My King, here I am.'

The king could hardly believe his ears.

'Yes, I am here.'

Daniel's voice was clear and strong.

The king was full of joy.

'Daniel! Daniel! Who saved you? Are you hurt?'

'My lord King, God sent his angel to shut the lions' mouths and to tame them. Do not worry. I am not hurt.'

'Daniel, you are the servant of the only living God,' cried the king.

His voice brought soldiers and guards running. At first they could not grasp what had happened. Open-mouthed, they stood there.

'Don't stand there,' the king ordered. 'Push the stone aside and let Daniel out.'

The princes and governors were also anxious to discover what had happened to Daniel.

They had been feasting all night.

Their enemy, Daniel, was dead.

'Perhaps the lions will have left a few bones for our dogs,' they mocked.

Raucously, they made their way to the den.

A vast crowd of people had gathered before it.

Now they could hear the king's voice ring out:

'Daniel's God is to be worshipped throughout my kingdom. He is the living God. His kingdom is eternal and his might never ends.'

'Long live the King! Long live Daniel!'

The shout hit the men like a sword-thrust.

They stood there paralyzed, dumb with shock.

Daniel was still alive!

'Flee!' called one of them.

But he was too late. The king had seen them.

'Bring them here,' he ordered.

Their wails and protestations of innocence filled the square.

'Your laments are in vain,' said the king. 'You are not even worth speaking to. The trap which you set for Daniel and myself will now prove to be your own undoing.'

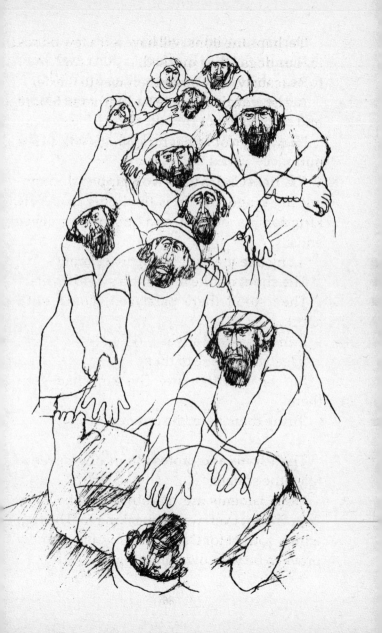

Darius showed no mercy.

'Throw them to the lions! I don't ever want to hear their flattering voices again.'

In the sight of the crowd they were seized and thrown down into the den.

'Shall we roll the stone back in front of the entrance?' asked the soldiers.

'No, there is no need for any stone.'

7

Cyrus, the Persian king, was amazed when he heard what had happened in the lions' den in Babylon.

'What sort of man can he be?' he wondered. During a visit to Babylon he called Daniel into his presence.

Still upright, but now with white hair, the prophet stood before him. He was nearly eighty years old.

'Tell me something about your life,' the king asked him.

Daniel lost all sense of time.

Once more his life lay spread out before him: his childhood in Jerusalem, the night when he had been captured, his first years in a strange country, the miracle in the burning, fiery furnace, Nebuchadnezzar's terrible illness, Belshazzar and the writing on the wall.

He also told him about Jeremiah and his promise and about his fellow countrymen, the prisoners. Over the years many of them had died and the children knew about their homeland only by hearsay.

Fifty years had passed since Jerusalem had been destroyed. But the longing to return was as bitter as on the first day.

The king did not forget Daniel's words. He worried about the fate of these people and he felt sympathetic towards them.

He asked to see maps of Jerusalem and plans of the ruined temple. He studied the customs and traditions of the Jews. His scholars were ordered to tell him the history of the Jewish kings and the sayings of the prophets.

Their great faith in an invisible god moved him.

He came to a definite decision.

Daniel was one of the first to hear it.

'Daniel,' said Cyrus, 'your invisible God has chosen me. You may return to your homeland. The temple in Jerusalem is to be rebuilt at the king's expense. I will give the holy treasure back to your people.'

Daniel fell to his knees and prayed:

'God is mighty,
He changes time and hour when he wishes.
He causes kings to fall and kings to rise.
He grants us wisdom and understanding.
He knows all that is secret and hidden.
He knows what lies behind the darkness.
I thank you and praise you, O Lord my God.'

The king's edict filled the prisoners with joy and excitement.

Sheshbazzar, a brave Judean, was to lead the journey back.

The way was long. The journey from Babylon to Jerusalem was over 1,000 miles.

The preparations took weeks.

Some people decided to stay in Babylon.

The king left it to them to decide. They had started businesses and achieved high office and wealth. The country had become their homeland.

Many of them were old. They could not embark on such an arduous journey.

And Daniel?

He sensed that his life was nearing its end, that he had fulfilled the task which God had given him.

'Come with us,' said the returning people. 'We will provide a carriage for you.'

Daniel smiled.

'My greatest wish has been fulfilled. I shall stay here but my heart will travel with you.'

He gave Sheshbazzar a scroll.

'Look after it well,' he said. 'Place it in the new temple at Jerusalem.'

It was Jeremiah's message.

The day of departure dawned.

It was spring.

Already, during the night, the travellers had collected together in groups. As soon as the sun rose, the long column slowly began to move.

People stood at the windows — curious people, friends, and relatives. They waved to the travellers and threw flowers at them.

The column seemed never-ending. There were thousands of people, whole families with their menservants and maids, and among them went the animals carrying provisions and furniture, mules, horses and camels. In the villages and small towns more

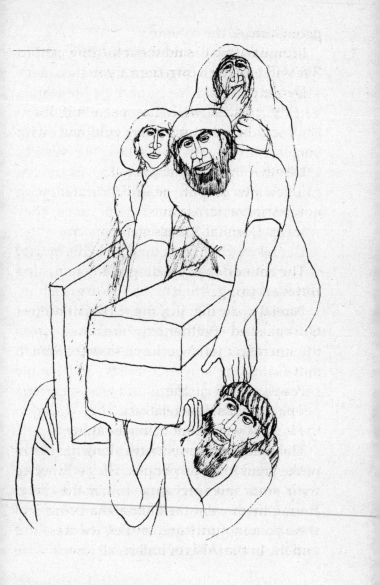

people joined the column.

In front went the musicians. They carried lyres and harps slung from their shoulders. They sang the old songs of their homeland. After the musicians came the carts containing the holy treasure: thirty gold and silver basins, thirty gold and 400 silver vessels, 1,000 other cups, twenty-nine knives and ten candlesticks of pure gold, decorated with golden flowers. As in ancient times, they were to adorn the temple in Jerusalem.

Daniel watched from the roof of his house.

The column kept pausing as the returning travellers stopped and looked up to greet him.

Daniel knew many of them, the children of Gibbar and Bethlehem, the men from Michmas and Jericho, the children of Ramah and Gaba, the singers, priests, and temple servants from Jerusalem.

The tears ran down his face.

He went with them in his thoughts.

Now they will travel north along the banks of the great River Euphrates. They will set up their tents and sing songs round the camp-fires. One day they will cross the borders of their home country and see the Sea of Galilee and the brown hills of Judah . . .

Daniel did not notice that the sun had long ago risen high overhead, that it scorched down, and that his feet were tired from standing so many hours.

Far outside the town the dust hung like a cloud over the column of people.

Suddenly someone laid a hand on his shoulder.

Startled, Daniel woke from his dreams.

'Hananiah! Mishael and Azariah! It is you!'

He smiled.

They, too, had grown old. They, too, had white hair. Mishael limped, and had to lean upon a stick.

'Yes, we are here,' they said. 'We shall stay with you.'